God Is No Island

God
IS
No Island

OSWALD C. J. HOFFMANN

Concordia Publishing House

Saint Louis　　London

NOTE. Quotations from the Scriptures are from a number of versions, including the King James Version, the Revised Standard Version, the New English Bible, and J. B. Phillips' paraphrase, to bring out the force of the original.

Second Printing 1969

Concordia Publishing House, St. Louis, Missouri
Concordia Publishing House Ltd., London, E. C. 1
© 1969 Concordia Publishing House
Library of Congress Catalog Card No. 71-80998

MANUFACTURED IN THE UNITED STATES OF AMERICA

Preface

Things are coming unhinged in this world of ours. Racial prejudice is escalating into racial violence. Freedom to be a good neighbor is often turned into license to do what one pleases without regard for others. The great god Success captivates the minds of some and has become the broken idol of failure for others who were once affluent and powerful.

Church members have forgotten the call of their Master to "come and die" as His disciples. Parents care less about the character of their children than the comforts of their pet animals. Science and technology have replaced God and the practice of religion for many. The youth cult in our generation has made our aging population look silly in its attempt to look and act young. The appeal of communism has misled many to overlook its anti-God and anti-man philosophy. Confusion over political developments has created a new pessimism about ordered government in society.

The bad in the world has always caused "hang-ups" for the people of God. It is easy to wring hands in despair and raise arms in holy horror, to join the chorus of defeatists who chant, "What is this world coming to!" Too many church people all over the world are content to chant and let it go at that. They lament the turn of events, crawl into their little shelters, and wait for the church to die and its message to die away.

Where is our faith? Our generation isn't the first to face unbelief, despair, persecution, violence, cruelty, disorder, war, poverty, and all the other ills of men. God has not withdrawn from His world. He was with Israel in the slime pits and slave huts of Egypt. He was with His people in famine and war and captivity. He was with His men when apostles suffered in chains and faithful believers died by the sword or in the games Romans played. He was in His world when thousands died of the plague in Europe and when millions of bodies were piled up by futile wars since that time.

Things may look bad, but God has not abdicated, nor has He gone on Medicare. God is not detached from the suffering and crime and evil of men in our time. God is not an island, living by Himself and unconcerned with the troubles of men today. God could have refused to involve Himself in the confusion we have in His world, but He did not fail us. He made this world and all its people. He could not let His creation go. He sent His Son, Jesus Christ, to become a Man among men in our world. Jesus came to tie men to God again, giving Himself into suffering and death for the sins of the world, and rising in powerful victory over every evil that man and Satan could devise. All is going for us, in Christ.

God is not an island, and we cannot be content to withdraw and complain about the world's evils. God is not an island, and the Gospel of Jesus Christ must be proclaimed with more urgency and power than ever before. Believers in Christ must be challenged to tell boldly the Good News that Christ died for their sins according to the Scriptures and that He was raised again as the Lord of all. In the Gospel of Christ resides the power to mount a vigorous attack on the satanic forces that cause misery, hatred, prejudice, selfishness, emptiness, and all the other evils of our world.

This is no time for pessimism or defeatism. The evils in our world cry out for the Word of Christ. These are times of opportunity to bring the Good News of Christ to the nations.

Contents

1

No Man an Island

"No man is an island, entire of itself. Every man is a piece of the continent, a part of the main. . . . Any man's death diminishes me, because I am involved in mankind; and therefore never send to know for whom the bell tolls; it tolls for thee."

These striking words, which have inspired a song and given a title to a well-known novel, come from the pen of an English preacher, John Donne. They call the world back from an extreme individualism, so rampant and rugged, so far removed from reality, that it has gone wild. In an age in which people have become accustomed to say, "I can do as I please," or "I don't care what others do as long as they don't hurt me," we must be reminded that no man lives for himself alone or dies for himself alone. None of us is that self-sufficient. And, said St. Paul, if we knew the God who has made us and redeemed us, none of us would want to be! "No one of us lives, and equally no one of us dies, for himself alone." (Rom. 14:7)

No man is an island of privilege, and no man is an island of responsibility. It is not possible for any one of us to say, "It's my life, my body, my mind to do with as I please — after all, I am the only one involved," or " — I and the next fellow are the only ones involved."

Whether we like it or not, every one of us is involved with others in more ways than we like to admit. Still, there are those who will go to almost desperate lengths to avoid recognizing the fact. I have heard about a father who accidentally hit a boy on the street with his car. A crowd gathered. The man picked up the boy, put him in his car, and said he was going to take him to a hospital. Five blocks away he heartlessly put the seriously injured boy out on the street because he did not want to become involved. Of course, he *was* involved. Before he was finished he had involved his whole family, his friends, his business associates, and many other people in the ruin that came to his own life, his financial resources, and his reputation.

Attempting to avoid involvement often results in hopeless involvement. Trying to get away from his troubles, a man turns to alcohol. The final result is that he is hopelessly involved himself and has involved everybody around him in his troubles, for an alcoholic never suffers alone.

A girl gets involved with a man. Having transgressed the law of God and the canons of society, she finds herself with child, which will have to be born out of wedlock. Instead of turning to her parents for help, the logical thing to do, she makes an effort to conceal everything by taking desperate measures that result in her own death. The end of that road is bitterness for everyone concerned, especially for those who are most involved in her life and are most deeply grieved by what has happened to her.

Whole nations have been known to suffer for the wilfulness of one man or a little group of men determined to rule at whatever price. The whole world is still paying for the sins of Adolf Hitler and Joseph Stalin. The whole world will pay for the actions of any man who begins a nuclear war. The whole world is still paying for the sin of the first man, whose defiance of God has muddied the whole stream of life.

The proof of this fact is before our eyes every day. It is a fact that through one man sin entered into the world and through sin death, pervading the whole human race to the point where every man is a sinner subject to death both by inheritance and by disposition. All of us are involved, unfortunately, and all of us are involved together. There is a solidarity that unites us all, a solidarity of rebellion against God and of unwillingness to walk His way. Wishing to avoid involvement, many people simply refuse to face the facts, closing their ears to the voice of conscience, closing their minds and hearts to the voice of God, and some even closing their eyes to the very existence of God.

13

Instead of providing release from involvement, this process only involves a man hopelessly in a destiny that is bitter to the heart of God Himself—the death of a sinner.

God is not an island. Fortunately for us this is true. He could have refused to become involved in the mess we have made of His world, but He did not. He could have avoided entanglement, but He did not. With deliberate forethought the God who made this world, and made it right, involved Himself in the affairs of men, who had gone wrong. Compelled only by love—the greatest compulsion there is in our selfish world—He took a hand to redeem His rebellious children and bring them back into His family.

This, this alone, explains why Jesus Christ, the Son of God, became a Man. It explains why He lived as He did and why He died as He did. It explains why He was raised from the dead by the glory of His Father. All this happened because the grace and love of God could not bear to see men going to their destined end with no way out. By the grace of God there is a way out. "If the wrongdoing of that one man brought death upon so many, its effect is vastly exceeded by the grace of God and the gift that came to so many by the grace of the one Man, Jesus Christ. . . . As the issue of one misdeed was condemnation for all men, so the issue of one just act of this Man Jesus Christ means acquittal and life for all men. For

14

as through the disobedience of the one man the many were made sinners, so through the obedience of the one Man the many will be made righteous." (Rom. 5:15, 18-19)

When Jesus Christ came, God was involved. When Christ died, God was involved. When Jesus Christ rose from the dead, God was involved. In Christ, God involved Himself freely and willingly in the tragic history of mankind. In this one life and this one death, you are involved whether you acknowledge the fact or not. Christ lived for you and died for you. You can't *make* it true, because it *is* true. What is true you can make your own by accepting Jesus Christ as your Savior. The moment you say of Christ, "He is for me," you have accepted Him. To accept Him that way by faith is to become involved with the living God, and what an involvement that is!

Involvement with God by faith in Christ is often treated in this skeptical world of ours as if it really represented an attempt to escape from life. The fact that he accepts Christ's atonement for sin has been thrown up to many a believer as if he were trying to escape from responsibility for his misdeeds. The reverse is true. A believer in Christ *does* accept responsibility for whatever he has done amiss. It is just this feeling of guilt and of sorrow for sin that causes him to turn to the forgiveness of God, freely provided in Jesus Christ. The believer feels personally involved in the death of

Christ because he is personally responsible for it. What is more, by faith in Christ he becomes personally involved in an altogether new way of life that makes far greater demands on him than he would possibly recognize or accept if he were not associated with Christ.

No man is an island. Far from letting responsibility go unrecognized, the Christian faith calls every believer to responsible fulfillment of duty. No man is an island. "None of us lives to himself, and no man dies to himself. For whether we live, we live unto the Lord; and whether we die, we die unto the Lord; whether we live, therefore, or die, we are the Lord's. For to this end Christ both died and rose, and revived, that He might be Lord both of the dead and living." (Rom. 14:7-9)

To become involved with Christ by faith is to be involved with all mankind. From the moment I come to know Christ as my Savior, every man's suffering is my suffering, every man's dying is my dying. Every child's gnawing hunger strikes my heart, and every man's slavery is a matter of concern to me too. The sufferings of the oppressed Czechs, Chinese, and East Germans are my problem too. I am not free to go my way unconcerned when my brother, who has been redeemed by Christ, is not free.

No man is an island of suffering. We are part of the misery and sickness of the human race.

Those who lie on beds of pain are part of me. As long as they suffer, I cannot be entirely happy; as long as they are sick, I cannot be entirely whole. I am involved with them through Christ by faith; being involved with Him, I am involved with the whole needy world.

There are differences between people. You don't have to be a preacher to see that. There are rich and poor, weak and strong, intelligent and not so intelligent, beautiful and not so beautiful. People come in all shapes and sizes and in a lot of different colors. There are men and women, boys and girls. God is not running a production line, like Ford or General Motors, where each human being comes off looking exactly like the other. Individuality is the mark of God's personality. The individuality of humanity is the uniqueness and originality of God Himself shining through His creation. God made people to be different. He never intended these differences, however, to be used as they are being used — as a club, a weapon, or a means of exploiting one another. God-given differences were intended to be used for the common good that people might help one another, that they might complement one another. The disorder in the world, accentuated by the differences between people, does not come from God. It is rather a sign of separation from God — the state of sin in which a man sets up housekeep-

17

ing for himself, divorces himself from God, and says, "I can live by myself, on my own resources, and for myself."

Christ came to heal the brokenness of humanity, to remove the root cause of the disorder troubling humanity. It is Christ's purpose to transform the end result of the world disorder, which is death, into its very opposite, which is life. Becoming involved with Christ by faith, following His plan and purpose, I am called upon to live a new life. I cannot allow the fact that I am different from someone else to become a source of pride and conceit. I cannot yield to that type of individualism that treats another man's weakness or sickness or sorrow as if it were of no concern to me. I cannot give myself to the hatreds and prejudices that arise from the separateness of men.

The cross of Christ is meant to heal all that, to bind up the brokenhearted and to bring together the shattered pieces of life. The redemption of Christ has as its goal the restoring of unity and wholeness to life, the rejoining of a man to his God in a relationship of trust and confidence and to his fellowman in love and consideration.

The healing of the cross is going on all the time. Faith in Christ, nourished through the Word of God, is doing the job. In the process of proclaiming the Word of God, the church fulfills its role by which men may come to know who they are and act in accord with their identity—the redeemed of God through Jesus Christ.

Every day you hear decent, well-meaning people restating the position of Cain—"Am I my brother's keeper?"—in such clichés as, "I don't want to get mixed up in it," or "It's not my affair." Statements like these tell us something about the time in which we live. People are too fearful of hurt or rebuff to become involved in the lives of others. There is no other way, however, if you would live as God would have you live.

You can make a real contribution to our time by living as God would have you live. Becoming involved with God means taking a chance. Becoming involved with Christ means taking a chance on Him. Take that chance. You will not be disappointed. Taking your chances with Christ, you will have to take your chances with a lot of other people who live around you.

Getting involved with other people always means taking a chance, as Morton Hunt has pointed out in an article published by *Reader's Digest:* "The person you fall in love with may hurt you terribly, the quarreling friends you try to reconcile may turn their joint anger upon you, the drowning man you try to save may pull you under with him. Yet in avoiding hurts and disappointments we become cold, inhuman." In his book *The Four Loves,* C. S. Lewis says: "If you want to make sure of keeping it intact, you must give your heart to no one, not even to an animal. Avoid all entanglements, lock it up safe in the coffin of your selfishness. In that casket—safe, dark, motionless, airless—it will not change. It will not be broken; it will become unbreakable, impenetrable, irredeemable."

The faith of Christ calls us to another kind of life—with soft heart and hard head—that forces us to admit and act upon what has always been true: "God is not an island, and no man is an island."

2

Is God White?

St. Paul's preaching did not please everybody. He preached the cross of Jesus Christ atoning for the sins of the whole world. The preaching of the cross, as the apostle himself said, proved to be a genuine stumbling block for the religious legalists among his own people and was looked on generally as a misguided and misleading mysticism by the dominant intellectual group setting the cultural climate of that time.

Unpopular with the religionists and with the eggheads, the apostle found himself in conflict also with people who claimed to be his followers, professing faith in the Christ whom he preached. Their faith, such as it was, had little effect on their pride and prejudices—a fact the apostle was not ready to overlook. Faith in Christ works, he said. It works in such a revolutionary way that any man who is in Christ will be a new creation. When a man truly follows Christ, the old disappears, and behold, all things become new.

This was not popular doctrine then, and it is not popular now. Still, the truth must be told. Anyone who preaches in the apostolic tradition must proclaim the whole counsel of God—and this is part of it, an important part! Once a man has come to faith in Christ, for him there is no longer either Jew or Greek; there is neither slave nor free; there is neither male nor female; for *all are one in Christ Jesus.*

"Ye are all the children of God by faith in Christ Jesus," said Paul, "for as many of you as have been baptized into Christ have put on Christ. There is neither Jew nor Greek, there is neither bond nor free, there is neither male nor female; for *ye are all one in Christ Jesus.*" (Gal. 3:26-28)

"God is white!" This is the sarcastic indictment of a character in one of Jean Genet's plays. The remark is meant to be a stinging indictment of the whole Western World, Christian and non-Christian alike, which has all too often acted on the ridiculous assumption that God is white—or at least displays a noticeable preference for white people. From the savage plundering of the slave-running days to the present piety of the pre-empted pew, our ancestors and a good many of us today have acquired the notion that God is partial to people with white skin. In a ludicrous effort to make God in our own image, we have actually convinced ourselves that God plays favorites with some of us.

The situation is further complicated by the fact that some black people are sure that God is black, and some yellow people insist He is yellow, as there must be some red people who think of Him as purely red. The political Reds of the Hammer and Sickle, of course, brazenly proclaim there is no God, assuring the world that they themselves are gods and calling on the nations to follow them to the heaven on earth they promise to establish.

The actual fact is that God shows no partiality. He is no respecter of persons. God is not red; He is not red, white, and blue; nor is He red, white, and black. He is God with His own hue, having shown His colors in His own way on a cross outside a city wall.

In the shadow of that cross we all stand condemned. In the light of God's grace shining forth from the cross of Christ, we are all redeemed through the atoning blood of Christ, God's Son. We all need a Savior, and we all have a Savior in Christ the Lord, whether we belong to the one third of the world's population that is white or to the two thirds of the world's population that is colored.

The great God who made this world of ours opened His heart to all men through His Son, who became a Man in our behalf. There is only one way to the heart of God—by faith in Jesus Christ. Faith in the unique and eternal Son of God makes a man a son of God. This is no joke. The apostle means what he says: "Ye are all the children of God by faith in Christ Jesus."

Faith in Christ always has been revolutionary. It has always had the effect of revolutionizing the lives of people previously devoted to preserving a miserable status quo based on inherited antagonisms and traditional prejudices. Faith in Christ was revolutionary in the apostolic age, when some people prided themselves on being Jews and others on being Greeks, some enjoyed the distinction of being free while others were saddled with all the disadvantages of being slaves, and men had all the privileges and the property while women were looked on as chattels. With the advent of the faith of Christ, all this changed. Children of God, born through faith in Christ Jesus and baptized into Christ, had to see the whole world in a different light: "There is neither Jew nor Greek, there is neither bond nor free, there is neither male nor female"; *we are all one in Christ Jesus.*

Hardly a day passes without some news of an incident illustrating the fact that our world is not following the way of Christ. In Asia, Europe, Africa, or the Americas, someone is being treated badly simply because of his national origin or the color of his skin. Second-class citizenship is not unknown wherever there are certain supposed first-class citizens who wish to preserve privileges they think they have a right to enjoy simply because of their own national origin or the color of their skin.

One way to attack this problem, of course, is to spend a lot of time exploding the various myths of racial superiority. The trouble with this approach is that it never ends. When one Hitler dies with his own theories of racial superiority, another Hitler arises somewhere else in the world. When it comes to this massive problem of racial prejudice, reason alone never seems to supply the final solution. Reason does not turn people inside out, and it never will. Reason can show people the light, but it has never demonstrated its capacity to induce them to follow the light. Men are men, with all the cruelty and selfishness of which men are capable. Men are men, as they want themselves to be. Only God, apparently, can take a man and make of him what He wants a man to be.

It is not God's design that men should go through life full of pride, walking out on their Creator, at odds with God and with their fellowmen. It was not God's plan that men should conduct their affairs in a spirit of envy, pride, and conflict, constantly subjected to those deep-seated emotions we call "prejudice."

Prejudice is a family—it is not a hermit. The disposition that causes one man to hate and kill his neighbor is the same root evil that disposes another to snub his fellowman and another to look down on a whole race of people just because they are different.

Racial discrimination, whatever else it may be, is always a sin. It is a vice of intellect and will. It is a blasphemy against the one God, who created all and redeemed all through the death and resurrection of His Son. It is blatant rejection of God's will that we live together as His children and Jesus' brethren.

Feeding on pride, prejudice distorts and twists the humanity of everyone who harbors and fosters it. Because prejudice sits in judgment without love, because it attempts to justify itself at the expense of others, it is a fierce evil that finds deep root in the basically selfish character of all men. It was to this our Lord spoke: "The judgment you give will be the judgment you get." (Matt. 7:2)

Speaking to professing Christians who had not yet fully learned what it means to be truly Christian, St. James wrote: "My brethren, show no partiality as you hold the faith of our Lord Jesus Christ, the Lord of glory. For if a man with gold rings and in fine clothing comes into your assembly, and a poor man in shabby clothing also comes in, and you pay attention to the one who wears the fine clothing and say, 'Have a seat here, please,' while you say to the poor man, 'Stand there,' or, 'Sit at my feet,' have you not made distinctions among yourselves and become judges with evil thoughts? . . . If you really fulfill the royal Law, according to the Scripture, 'You shall love your neighbor as yourself,' you do well. But if you show partiality, you commit sin and are convicted by the Law as transgressors." (2:1-4, 8-9)

Here there can be no compromise. This has to do with the nature of God. God is not white or black or yellow or red. He refuses to play favorites. He refuses to let His people play favorites. St. James was just echoing the theology of Paul: Faith in Christ and the old prejudices cannot live side by side. "There is neither Jew nor Greek, there is neither slave nor free, there is neither male nor female; for *ye are all one in Christ Jesus.*"

In the family of God, populated by those who have become the children of God by faith in Jesus Christ, there is no room for the prejudicial judgments that are so common in our world as almost to be taken for granted. Faith in Christ does not permit a man to take anything for granted — except the love of God, which shows no partiality at all.

In the family of God men do not cease being men, and women do not cease being women. Blacks are still blacks, and whites are still whites. But it doesn't make any real difference at all. *All are one in Christ Jesus.*

The apostle Paul would have something to say about churches that violate the clear witness of the Scriptures in this important regard. They do so at their own peril and at the fearful price of capitulation to the world. When the church

27

acts as the world does, it is no longer the light of the world. Instead the world is squeezing the church into its own twisted mold, preventing Christians from hearing the clear Word of God and from showing forth the love of God to their fellowmen.

Let me be very clear on this point: Whenever a church refuses to welcome and win people because of their racial or cultural background, that church crucifies anew the Lord of glory to whom she pays lip service. Whenever the church concentrates its attention on the people in the suburbs and forgets the people in the great cities, it is becoming secular in its outlook, forgetting the Great Commission to go and make disciples of all nations. Whenever Christian people forget to be friendly to people who are different, they leave behind the Lord of glory, who has bought them and all men with a great price.

During the heyday of the Nazis in Germany, so the story goes, a Nazi Storm Trooper entered a large German church one Sunday morning and interrupted the service of worship by announcing: "Will all those of Jewish background leave immediately!" There was breathless silence. Again the voice thundered: "All those of Jewish background leave at once!" Again there was silence — until to the astonishment of all, the figure of Christ above the altar climbed down off the cross and made His exit.

28

Of course, this story never happened. But it does remind us of something our Lord said: "Inasmuch as you did it — or did it not — to one of the least of these My brothers, you did it — or did it not — to Me" (see Matt. 25:31-46). The meaning of His words could not be plainer.

In Christ, God acted to atone for the sins of all men. He had every reason to exact judgment from each of us, but He put the whole burden of that judgment on His own Son. Jesus Christ went to the cross to bear the full brunt of human prejudice and pride; in His resurrection there is power for the whole world to be redeemed and restored from its pride. There is forgiveness of sins in Christ, the gift of freedom from both the guilt of sin and the punishment for sin. There is strength for a new life in Christ, a life in harmony with the will of God. Christ has abolished segregation and discrimination, reconciling men of every tongue, kindred, people and nation "to God in one body through the cross, thereby bringing the hostility to an end." (Eph. 2:16)

The church is called "the body of Christ." It is a body of diversity and of newborn creativity, composed as it is of people who are dependent on one another as the organs of the body are dependent on one another. There are no superior or inferior members: *All are one in Christ.* The rustle of money, the cut of the clothes, the respectable name, the color of skin — all these are insignificant. Christ died to free us from these inane values—that we might be persons again, brothers of one family, all because of His cross!

To be baptized into Christ is no mere formality. To be baptized into Christ is to share the benefits of His death and the glory of His life. It is like being born again. It is like beginning life anew. It is like putting on a garment never worn before. "As many of you as have been baptized into Christ have put on Christ."

Once a man has put on Christ, there can be no turning back.

> Jesus, Thy blood and righteousness
> My beauty are, my glorious dress;
> Midst flaming worlds, in these arrayed,
> With joy shall I lift up my head.

That's not just talk! It is the authentic response of anyone and everyone who has truly experienced the love of God in Christ, which draws no lines at all and knows no boundaries at all.

Bear the cross with honor. In the cross, conquer! Forget the old, put on the new! Break loose from the web of suspicion and judgment and pride—whether you are on the giving or the receiving end—by faith in Jesus Christ. Crack the barrier! Know Christ and be free! In Him there is neither Jew nor Greek, there is neither bond nor free, there is neither male nor female; for *you are all one in Christ Jesus.*

3

The New Morality

Describing the moral situation of our time, one writer has said: "Something in the air has anesthetized the nerve of self-control, released the inner restraint, freed men of vital checks and balances. We are becoming the 'anything goes' generation."

Turning its attention to college campuses, *Newsweek* magazine described what it calls the new morality: "In its simplest terms, the new campus morality permits 'sex with love' provided that a girl doesn't fall in love with two people at the same time. Sex with anyone except 'Mr. Right' is largely frowned upon, as is out-and-out promiscuity. The question is, how many Mr. Rights make a wrong?"

Throwing about itself the cloak of modernity and freedom, the new morality sets itself up as a fresh and exciting standard to live by, especially for young people who want to break out of the old traditions and conventions. Actually, of course, this new morality is simply the old immorality in new dress.

In the fifth chapter of Galatians, St. Paul

described the old immorality in blunt and uncompromising terms, calling its characteristic products the works of the flesh: "Now the works of the flesh are plain: immorality, impurity, licentiousness, idolatry, sorcery, enmity, strife, jealousy, anger, selfishness, dissension, party spirit, envy, drunkenness, carousing, and the like."

At one American university several hundred students staged a 2-day demonstration to protest a new rule requiring that doors to dormitory rooms be kept open whenever a boy and girl are together inside. The student newspaper on this campus said, somewhat petulantly, that the new regulation "makes impossible any meaningful relationship between boy and girl." No matter how young this editor may have been, his editorial comment is both incredibly naive and downright arrogant. It ignores human nature, challenging not only the conventions that have been developed to protect young people from themselves but even the basis of upright human conduct itself.

This attitude, characteristic of the new morality, is not confined to young people. One New York hotel manager says that he does not care if an unmarried couple sign the register as man and wife. What does anger him is that a man takes a room as a single occupant and then brings a woman in—thus cheating the hotel of its revenue.

This morality of the gutter affects not only

the man in the street but also the man in the pew. A dedicated churchgoer recently told proudly of returning a five-dollar bill to a drugstore clerk who had given him too much change. When he completed a long-distance phone call from a pay booth, however, and the operator returned his five quarters by mistake, he kept the money without a qualm. "The phone company is so big," he said, "they won't miss it."

The more we talk about the new morality, the closer we get to home. What we are talking about is not just something we can criticize in others. It is a quality of life that touches us all. All of us have been tainted, to some extent, by the attraction of what we are sometimes disposed to call freedom, the right to do exactly as we please. So it happens that fathers are very strict with their boys but extremely lenient with themselves. Mothers decry the lack of social standards among the young people with whom their daughters associate, but they are not nearly so critical of the vicious gossip with which reputations are destroyed over the bridge table by their own associates.

It is a fact of modern life that many people who pride themselves on their uprightness employ the most venal and occasionally the most vicious means to accomplish their supposedly righteous ends. Attempts to achieve worthy ends through unworthy methods make wholesome morality look like a joke, often providing a plausible excuse for the outright revolt against accepted moral standards that is characteristic of the new morality.

When we criticize the new morality, let us be honest. Is it really true that in days gone by the hotel manager would not have tolerated the two who tried to register without being married, or that the recipient of the five quarters would have put them back immediately into the phone? Is it really true that formerly people were good and now they are bad? You know the answers to these questions as well as I do.

Something new has been added, however. The new morality, such as it is, insists that all morality is private in character. Whatever a man does in private is his own business. Whatever he decides to do in the privacy of his heart is his own concern. As a result, what would have been impossible or unthinkable in earlier days now is often accepted and practiced as altogether normal public behavior.

One of the deans of Harvard University charged that a "growing number of students" were taking dormitory visiting privileges as a "license to use the college rooms for wild parties or sexual intercourse." The *Harvard Crimson*, the student newspaper, replied that sexual freedom is similar to freedom of religion and of speech, that is, a matter of individuality subject only to

34

private standards of conduct. Every man must decide for himself what is right, and that is that.

This idea extends to every area of human conduct today. What is right is right, as long as one has decided that it is all right for him. The dean of women at Radford College in Virginia conducted a study to determine why students cheat. She concluded that there is not only a "massive increase in cheating in all phases of education" but "what is worse, a shift in attitude towards cheating." Students appear to assume that individual misbehavior is of no social consequence as long as no one gets hurt. Whole books have been written to justify this outlook on life.

The move of people from the country to the cities, which is going on all over the world, has helped people throw off the old restraints against immorality in the areas of sex, business ethics, personal conduct, ambition, and prejudice. In the cities you can find the means to do what you want to do. People can sin and get away with it. No one is watching. No one stands over them to censor them. More important—no one seems to care.

The obvious result of this privatist ethic is an increase in crime, which costs people in the United States alone at least 27 billion dollars a year. That's eight times more than all Americans of all faiths give for religious purposes at home and abroad. Newspapers, radio, and television are filled with stories about murders, muggings, rapes, houses burglarized, and cars stolen. The result is that many cities are becoming jungles, and people are appalled.

Now we see the strange anomaly. Changes in private morality have been greeted with tolerance and in some cases with cheers. Because in the modern world people have the freedom to make choices in areas of power, money, and influence, it is assumed that they also have the right to make similar choices when it comes to sex, prejudice, and personal morality. Often the same people who insist we must find a new moral code that will fit the needs of the society we live in are calling for more stringent action against public immorality and the violent crimes that usually accompany it.

We cannot have our cake and eat it too. The new morality, with all its plea for personal freedom and self-assertion, is an invitation to self-indulgence. This is what you get when you develop a standard of personal morals that permits people to do anything they can get away with. This is not new. It is old. It is the old immorality described by St. Paul: "Anyone can see the kind of behavior that belongs to the lower nature: fornication, impurity, and indecency; idolatry and sorcery; quarrels, a contentious temper, envy, fits of rage, selfish ambitions, dissensions, party intrigues, and jealousies; drinking bouts, orgies, and the

36

like. I warn you, as I warned you before, that those who behave in such ways will never inherit the kingdom of God." (Gal. 5:19-21)

St. Paul was not a bluenose or a prude. He was not trying to impose on other people some moral code of his own. He was simply telling people what the will of God is for their own well-being. When it comes to public or private morality, God will have His say. This is what He says: No one who gives himself to a privatistic ethic that pays no attention to the will of God is going to get away with it.

Men cannot be men and women cannot be women without discipline and self-restraint. People who think it is open-minded to live without regard for the will of God had better be careful that their brains don't fall out.

Twenty years ago, in his *Values for Survival*, Lewis Mumford wrote: "For the last 200 years a long succession of thinkers, from Diderot and Rousseau onward, have urged man to throw off his ancient taboos: to act on his impulses, yield to his desires, abandon measure in his gratifications." Mumford warned that the sweet voices of relaxation lure us toward disaster. He went on to remind us that man is neither wholly rational nor wholly good, and insisted that in man there is a demonic nature that must be kept in chains.

This is hard for modern man to take, but it is true. Because it is true, restraint is not neces-

37

sarily bad. The commandments still say, "Thou shalt not," and no one has yet been able to change them into a softer "Perhaps it would be better if you didn't."

On this score, St. Paul is uncompromising: "Now the works of the flesh are plain. . . .

"But the fruit of the Spirit is love, joy, peace, patience, kindness, goodness, faithfulness, gentleness, self-control; against such there is no law. And those who belong to Christ Jesus have crucified the flesh with its passions and desires." (Gal. 5:22-24)

St. Paul's answer to the new morality is not negative but positive. You people who think you have found freedom in doing what you please, defying the will of God in the doing, have only delivered yourselves to a slavery more oppressive than the one you are trying to escape. To that slavery there is only one answer. The answer is Christ Jesus.

St. Paul's answer is not impractical. Jesus Christ knew life and what it is all about. He tasted life to the full. Like any man, He endured temptation; but He came through unscathed. He suffered what life has to offer. He suffered once, the Just for the unjust, to bring us to God. This is atonement. He suffered for us, paying the price for our sins; and He invites everyone to follow Him.

Following Christ takes faith. You have to trust Christ that He is what He claimed to be, the Son of God and the Savior of the world. You must have confidence that there is forgiveness of sins in Him. This is His way: accept His forgiveness, and go His way.

The way of Christ is perfect freedom — freedom from the restraints imposed by the works of the flesh, freedom to enjoy the fruit of the Spirit — in other words, freedom for everything that makes life positively useful and wholesomely satisfying.

Following Christ will not take the fun out of life. It will keep you from getting hurt. Following Christ in faith makes life worth living. It will not be heaven on earth but it will not be hell either. The works of the flesh create a hell on earth; the fruit of the Spirit gives a taste of heaven.

If you could read some of the letters that pass over my desk, you would know what it means to have a broken heart or a broken home as the result of unfaithfulness or drunkenness or plain ordinary jealousy, anger, selfishness, and dissension. You would see what immorality, impurity, and licentiousness can do to a man or woman.

You don't have to go that way. There is always Christ. Christ is for you. Through faith in Christ, enjoy "the fruit of the Spirit: love, joy, peace, patience, kindness, goodness, faithfulness, gentleness, self-control; against such there is no law. And those who belong to Christ Jesus have crucified the flesh with its passions and desires."

God knows you. Whether you are young or old, God knows you very well. He knows who you are, and He knows what you need for a happy life. You will not really be yourself until you follow His will and go His way.

Do you feel frustrated and rebellious, not knowing which way to turn? Are you like some of my correspondents who tell me they feel all dirty inside because of what they have done? Let me tell you something: God forgives! He forgives for the sake of His Son, Jesus Christ. This is a fact. Accept it, and live by it. Live in the power of God's Spirit, who is touching your heart right now with the promptings of faith in Christ. In the power of the Spirit, take Christ into your heart. Let the Spirit lead you, by faith in Christ, to a life that is really free, filled with the fruit of the Spirit: love, joy, peace, patience, kindness, goodness, faithfulness, gentleness, and last but not least, self-control.

If you are looking for a new morality, my friend, promising freedom and giving victory, this is it. What it promises, it gives.

4

The Failure of Success

We Americans are supposed to be out-and-out materialists. The typical picture of an American in many parts of the world is that of a person who wears a dollar sign for a smile. It may be that Americans have contributed to that caricature by their own false standard of values, by their worship of success.

On the other hand, it may be that the critics are themselves overemphasizing the importance of material wealth and actually give it a higher place in their thinking than the people they criticize. Their bitter resentment may be the outgrowth of a way of thinking that regards material success as the end goal of all existence, the one objective that they have yet to achieve, the most important thing in life.

It is certain that the most violent critics of the American way of life, the representatives of communism throughout the world, have made things material their god. For communists, there is no good at all unless it is material good. There is no history unless it is interpreted in a material way. There is no power unless it is economic power. There is no success unless it is material success.

All this only points up the fact that all men, whoever they are and wherever they live, need to be reminded of a great truth in the Lord's words, recorded in Mark 8:36: "For what shall it profit a man if he shall gain the whole world and lose his own soul?"

Money cannot buy everything. Christ said: "Man does not live by bread alone." Advertising men on Madison Avenue in New York City and farmers on the roads of Iowa, businessmen in London and day laborers in Red China have found out through bitter experience that the words of the Lord are true. There are some things in life, important things, the value of which cannot be measured in terms of money or even in terms of the amount and quality of food on the table. That is a hard truth. Often the harder it is the truer it is.

"Nothing succeeds like success" is the slogan on which many people have built their lives. In every case, those are the people who are the living examples of the fact that success is not the only thing in life that is worthwhile. Indeed, it is often the cause of life's supreme failure. Success is like a petulant will-o'-the-wisp, which men pursue with passionate determination but can never quite catch, a pursuit that ends too often only in ulcers, frustration, defeat, and despair.

The financial successes of the 1920s were followed by the greatest flurry of suicides of successful men in the history of the world. The greatest success stories are often the greatest tragedies.

Judged by the commonly accepted standards of success, the story of the life of Jesus Christ reads like the story of a failure, tragic and complete. Born in the humblest of circumstances, He became a carpenter's son, only to desert the profession of His father and become an itinerant preacher. It has never been recorded of Him that He handled money. Nor is it ever said of Him that He carried a spare garment on His journeys. Thousands gathered to hear Him, of course, and were eager to listen to Him. Yet when He was taken into custody by the authorities, not only did the crowd who so eagerly hung on His words desert Him, but even His closest, most intimate friends turned their backs on Him. To a man, they forsook Him and fled.

He did not own an automobile. In fact, He very likely did not even own a beast of burden. One was requisitioned for Him that He might ride after a fashion in His triumphal entry into Jerusalem. Do you call that success? If it is, it certainly is a different kind of success than most people look for today.

All this raises an important question: What is success? Is it the achievement of material wealth? Or is it promotion in business? Is a man a success when he becomes assistant vice-president? Or when he becomes vice-president? Or is it when he becomes president? What kind of yardstick can we use to determine whether one man is successful and another is not? Did Adolf Hitler have something when he wrote: "Success is the sole earthly judge of what is right and what is wrong"?

To all those who use the yardstick of wealth or position or reputation, the Word of God has something pointed to say: "Woe unto them that join house to house, that lay field to field, till there be no place, that they may be placed alone in the midst of the earth" (Is. 5:8). Those words of Isaiah are the complete statement of the failure of success, success that is measured purely in material terms.

People who are pressing forward to success as the one goal in their lives ought to ask themselves a few questions: What price do I have to pay personally for the success that I'm seeking? Do I have to sacrifice love, kindness, friendship, and trust? Do I have to give up the leisurely enjoyment of God's good things and consume all my time in doing what I think will mark me as a successful man? Do I have to pay the terrible price of altering or even sacrificing my moral and ethical principles? Do I have the right to deny to my family what is rightfully theirs? Do

I have the right to deprive God of what is rightfully His?

There are people who think that they have discharged their obligation to God by going to church for one hour of worship a week. Some don't even do that, of course. Others are reluctant to give up anything in the service of God, because all their time is required to reach success defined in purely material terms. No success story can be worth that price.

Are you possibly one of those people who recognize their obligation to God but give Him their service in a grouchy way, with a frown? This, of course, is practically no service at all. It is like trying to serve God and mammon at the same time. It is like paying one's respects to God while all the while worshiping at the altar of another god.

You may say, "What have you got against success anyway?" I haven't anything against success. Indeed, I admire the successful man as much as the next man does. At the same time, as God's messenger, I cannot fail to point out that success can become the most abject failure. What is it that makes success a failure? What is it that turns success from a blessing into a curse? Is it not that spirit of which Christ was speaking in this text when He said: "What shall it profit a man if he gain the whole world and lose his own soul?" Christ's standard for success was evidently dif-

45

ferent from the standards commonly employed in measuring much of life today.

On the very night our Lord was betrayed, His disciples fell to bickering again about who should be accounted the greatest in the kingdom of God. Our Lord's disciples were aware that He was going up to Jerusalem for something quite important.

While they were traveling, they started an argument about rank. At that point He turned to them and said: "You know that those who are supposed to rule over the Gentiles lord it over them, and their great men exercise authority over them. But it shall not be so among you; but whoever would be great among you must be your servant, and whoever would be first among you must be slave of all. For the Son of man also came not to be served but to serve and to give His life as a ransom for many." (Mark 10:42-45)

The nameless waiter does not look like a very important man compared to the successful man who sits down to dinner at a fashionable eating place. Yet our Lord was willing to take the place of that waiter. He preferred to demonstrate His greatness by serving. In everything He did, right down to the cross, and in everything He said, there was a consuming desire to serve.

The prophet Isaiah gave our Lord a great name: the Suffering Servant of the Lord. He served through suffering, the climax of which was reached on the cross of Calvary. He dedicated not merely a moment of His life but His whole life to serving mankind, to serving us. Because He was a man, and at the same time God's Son, this service has eternal validity for each of us. In it there lies forgiveness, divine forgiveness, and citizenship in His kingdom.

In Christ's kingdom he is the greatest who serves. This is not the kingdom in which people argue whether material success is the thing; but in this Kingdom they strive to serve God and their fellowmen. This was the new standard of success introduced by our Lord Jesus Christ and His suffering service. He has willed to us a Kingdom. In fact, He has made each of us kings and priests to reign with Him. Who could possibly want a higher rank? There is a power and a glory in this kind of success that surpasses the dreams, the wildest dreams, of men.

There is no defeat and no failure in this kind of success. It is the kind that leaves a pleasant taste in a man's mouth. It is not the reward of ambition and drive but is the gift of God in Jesus Christ.

What happens then to the urge to beat out the other fellow, based on the slogan "Nothing succeeds like success?" What happens to the drive to get the top dollar for every sale, to get the highest per-hour wages for every hour of work? I'll tell you what happens to it. It dies.

It has to die anyway, of course, even as the psalmist said: "Be not afraid when one becomes rich, when the glory of his house increases. For when he dies he will carry nothing away" (Ps. 49: 16-17). That's an involuntary kind of dying that no man can avoid. The kind our Lord advocated was a wilful kind of dying, a voluntary and deliberate substitution of His own standards of success for all the standards of success that the world has evolved otherwise. He that is chief is he that doth serve. He bids us compete with one another to see who can be the greatest and the most successful, but that competition has to be in the area of service. He that is chief is he that doth serve.

How can you serve unless you know *whom* you serve? It is possible to gain the whole world and lose the greatest of all — your own life. It is possible to find God and to gain everything that is worth having — your own life.

I am not speaking of some vague generality when I speak to you about God. I am speaking of the God and Father of our Lord Jesus Christ. God wants to be known to you, and for that reason He revealed Himself in the person of His Son, Jesus Christ. Christ gave Himself for you that you might be forgiven and might be counted one of God's children. Christ rose from the dead to be your living Lord. He wants you to depend on Him in faith, believe in Him, trust Him, and

48

give your whole life over to Him. It was this Christ who said: "What shall it profit a man if he shall gain the whole world and lose his own soul?"

The possibility of a successful life lies before you. What kind of success will it be? A success that consists of the temporary domination of others, or a success that consists in constant service to others? A success that is great in the eyes of men, or a success that is great in the eyes of God? A success that destroys, or one that is part of God's saving plan for you? Choose Christ's way, and I guarantee you that your life will not be a failure. It will be a success, a success crowned with the divine blessing of Christ our Lord Himself.

5

Painless Christianity

Science has done a great deal to eliminate or at least to neutralize pain. Painless dentistry has become almost a reality in certain parts of the world. Certainly the old horror of waiting for the inevitable in the anteroom of the dentist's office is not what it once was.

Though there may be plenty of pain before and after an operation, surgery itself is usually performed in painless fashion. The very fact that so much time and effort has been expended by science to do away with pain only emphasizes a reality clouding all life.

Science has done little to ease the pain of an infant whose stomach contractions indicate hunger and cause him to cry. Obviously science has not been able to ease the pain of paying taxes, which become only more painful as taxes go higher and higher.

The process of learning has always been painful, a fact stated long ago by a Greek philosopher in two words: *Mathein Pathein* — to learn is to suffer. Unfortunately the corollary of this truth — to suffer is to learn — is not always true, since some people refuse to learn even from their pain.

There is no particular virtue, of course, in seeking out pain for its own sake. Nevertheless, some ends in life cannot be gained without the painful sacrifices necessary in order to achieve them. For most people, a savings account, however small, is the result of the painful process of thrift. The practice of thrift becomes even more painful in an age when advertising dangles before buyers the pleasant prospects of easy time-payments. All too many people have discovered to their pain that following the easy way is often more painful through payment of interest and carrying charges than would have been the hard way of sacrificing and saving.

There is no easy way to the goals to which God calls each of us. Christ offered no painless Christianity when He said: "If any man will come after Me, let him deny himself, and take up his cross, and follow Me" (Matt. 16:24). Nor did St. Paul offer a painless way of faith in the first two verses of the 12th chapter of his epistle to the Romans: "I beseech you therefore, brethren, by the mercies of God, that ye present your bodies a living sacrifice, holy, acceptable unto God, which is your reasonable service. And be not conformed to this world; but be ye transformed by the renewing of your mind, that ye may prove what is that good and acceptable and perfect will of God."

St. Paul gave no encouragement to people to toy with faith and to persist in thinking that they are following the Christian way, though seeking to avoid the sacrifice and pain that cannot be avoided if one is to be a real Christian. Pain, self-denial, and sacrifice are unavoidable in the Christian life.

Of course there is a great deal of comfort in the Christian faith. The hymn writer was correct in saying of Christian faith: "Here is balm for all our woes." If in trouble you seek God, you will discover, as the prophet pointed out, that God comforts, as a mother stills her child. Christ said: "Come unto Me all ye that labor and are heavy laden, and I will give you rest" (Matt. 11:28). Are you carrying sorrows, care, and burdens? Christ stands ready to answer your plea for help. Through faith in Christ you will receive the help and strength He offers, and you will most certainly obtain peace, rest, and relief. No one else but Christ can make this promise, "I will give you rest," and keep it.

We misunderstand Christ, however, if we regard Christianity as merely a religion of comfort. It is also a religion of pain. A faith that costs nothing, suffers nothing, does nothing, and gives nothing is worth nothing. Real Christian faith calls on a person to stand up and be counted. In our easygoing world, standing up to be counted for Christ is not easy.

Christ Himself did not find life to be easy and painless. Birth into the world is sometimes called a "blessed event," although none but mother and child know how painful it really is. The birth of our Lord was a blessed event for the world, although no one but He knew how painful it really was. It is easy to be sentimental about Christmas, to think of the birth of Christ as a glamorous event, until one remembers the sacrifice our Lord made in order to become a man. It was a divine pain for the eternal God to be born as a little child and then to be ignored by great and small.

Consider the suffering our Lord endured in behalf of mankind. He had never done, said, or thought an evil thing in His whole lifetime. We may be able to say pleasant and kind things, while our minds are thinking the exact opposite. Not what comes out of the mouth but what is in mind and heart really counts. Christ, however, never had an evil thought. He never had reason to feel guilty about anything. In spite of all this, He felt the whole weight of sin, the burden of guilt for a world's transgression. He had never known a moment of separation from His Father, but separation too was His lot because He was the sin-bearer of all mankind.

Christ's death was not easy. He was executed. He knew He was going to die, and death came to Him at a known, given moment. When a person is old, the angel of death often muffles his wings and permits him to slip peacefully out of this world. Jesus Christ went to His death in full possession of His faculties. The robbers at His side were simply executed. The Lord of heaven and earth was mocked as He was dying. To Him they said: "If you are the Son of God, come down from the cross." The mockers seemed to say to Him: "God is just. He would not let you suffer and die if you were innocent." It was as if the devil were saying to Him: "You are mine."

During the last few hours of His suffering, the sun darkened and the earth trembled. If the troubled conscience shudders at the rustling of a wind-blown leaf, how much more terrible was the pain of this Sufferer when the sun was blotted out and the earth was shaken. How feeble are our attempts to understand His cry of pain: "My God, My God, why hast Thou forsaken Me?"

All this St. Paul remembered in the injunction to a world redeemed by that suffering: "I appeal to you therefore, brethren, by the mercies of God, to present your bodies as a living sacrifice." The mercies of God are exemplified by the cross of Christ. More than that, they are shared with the world in the cross of Christ. The gift of God is eternal life through our Lord Jesus Christ. That gift is yours to take right now, by acceptance of the historical fact that Christ died for you, as well as of God's gift of forgiveness and life through the pain and sacrifice of Jesus Christ.

To accept Christ is to accept responsibility for bearing His name. To be a Christian means to bear the name of Christ as a badge of honor, an honor that cannot be borne without the pain of sacrificing ourselves in His behalf.

Relationship to Christ is something like that of marriage. A woman gives up her name to accept the name of her husband. She gives up a great deal more if it is a real marriage: she gives up herself. A husband gives up a great deal to make of this new relationship a marriage. He is no longer free to do just what he wants to do. He has to work hard to provide a home for the family, clothes for the wife and children, furniture for the house. Most of all, if it is to be a real marriage, he must give up himself to his wife and to the home they have established together. A marriage will never be altogether successful unless husband and wife are prepared to give themselves up for each other.

Christ gave Himself up freely and fully for the whole world. Those who follow Him must be prepared to give themselves up freely and fully for Him. Christ does not want merely your money. He is not looking only for your service. Christ wants *you*—your life, your heart, your will. He wants you to say to Him: "Thy will be done on earth as it is in heaven."

To give one's self up to Christ is not a matter of resignation, as if to say: "If evil happens to me, let Thy will be done." It is rather to say: "Let Thy will be done in me on earth at all times, as it is done by the angels in heaven, cheerfully and perfectly." Christ wants you to present your whole life, even your body, as a living sacrifice to Him. He wants your hands to do His will. He wants your feet to walk His way. He wants your intellect for His cause. He wants your lips to witness to His name. He wants your self, all of you.

Christ wants His followers to be martyrs to His cause. People think of martyrs as giving up their lives in one great act of devotion. Actually, the great martyrs of the past prepared all their lives for that one great act of devotion by performing all the little acts of devotion that God called on them to make. They remembered the mercies of God and offered themselves constantly as living sacrifices.

The living sacrifice of the Christian life is spelled out by St. Paul: "Do not be conformed to this world, but be transformed by the renewal of your mind." If Christianity is simply a painless affair to you, of course these words will not mean much. If you take St. Paul seriously, you will begin to understand that painless Christianity is an impossibility.

One of the great weaknesses of the Christian church today is that cleancut distinctions between believers and unbelievers have been wiped out. Except for the fact that people go to church on Sunday, you would hardly be able to recognize that some of them are Christians. They use the same filthy words, laugh at the same smutty stories, and are just as dishonest as some of their neighbors. They are just as ill-tempered, vengeful, and worrisome as the rest of the people in their neighborhoods. To be a Christian is to be different—to be different when it really counts.

Some people seem to think that the great difference between Christians and non-Christians lies in whether they use lipstick or not, how they do their hair, the kind of clothes they wear, and certain other inconsequential practices. These differences are purely external. They do not indicate any real difference at all.

The real differences have to do with what lies inside a man. Does he conform to the world, or is he transformed by the Spirit of Christ? The way not to be conformed is to be transformed; transformation is something that happens deep down within a man. The Greek word *transformed* describes what happens when a caterpillar becomes a butterfly. It is a metamorphosis, an outward change from within.

No one can make a butterfly by pinning wings on a caterpillar. Neither can we transform ourselves by eliminating bad habits and taking on some good ones. If people are to be transformed, they must be changed within. Their minds, their inner selves must be changed. That which causes them to think and be what they are must be renewed. To be renewed by a living trust in Jesus Christ is to put one's self at God's disposal for His use as He knows best.

Some people have just enough religion to make them miserable and not enough to make them happy. They don't have enough religion to keep them from sinning, but enough to keep them from enjoying it. St. Paul calls for a different kind of religion, a deeply committed Christianity that affects not only a person's manners but his whole way of life. He urges Christians to sacrifice everything—their ambitions, their desires, and themselves—in remembrance of the mercies of God, which found their culmination in the sacrifices of God's own Son, Jesus Christ.

Most of us are willing to make sacrifices of one kind or another. We may sacrifice something for self-improvement, our families, our children, our home, our country. God appeals for the greatest sacrifice of all, yourself. He appeals to you to make that sacrifice out of remembrance of His mercy on you.

It is not sacrifice to put yourself at God's disposal and then withdraw if God does not ask you to do what you yourself want to do. God asks you to give yourself over to His eternal plan, to place yourself at His disposal to use when and where He wills.

God appeals; He does not command. God does not treat you as a little child, whom one commands. He treats you as a grown-up; He reasons with you. His reasoning, if you accept Christ's sacrifice as having been offered by God in your behalf, is absolutely incontrovertible. If you accept the mercies of God at all, present your body as a living sacrifice; don't be conformed to this world, but be transformed by the renewal of your mind that you may prove what is the will of God, what is good and acceptable and perfect.

6

Parents or Zoo Keepers?

On a certain weekend, 37 college students, young men and young women, were arrested in one of the leading hotels in Indianapolis, Indiana. If there had been sufficient manpower, the police department explained, at least 50 more could have been arrested while racing lightly clad through the nine floors of the hotel in what one of the policemen described as a full-blown "Roman orgy." According to news reports, the father of one of the girls involved in the episode, when informed that his daughter was under arrest, heaved a great sigh of relief and remarked, "Oh, is that all? I thought she had been in an accident or something!"

What do fathers and mothers think they are, anyway? Parents, or zoo keepers? What are they raising, children destined to become men and women with a moral sense of their own, or educated animals suitable only for public display behind iron bars and glass—to keep the public from getting hurt? Every age has had its share of juvenile mischief while boys and girls found their way through adolescence to young adulthood and finally to the intellectual and emotional maturity of fairly well-balanced and stable men and women. What I am talking about today is not mere juvenile mischief or even juvenile disregard for some of the stuffy conventions of society. I am speaking about open flouting of the laws of God and men, accompanied by blatant disdain on the part of young people for the elemental rights of their fellowmen, whether peers or superiors, often resulting in malicious destruction of property and all too frequently in physical death or injury for those with whom they come into contact at home or on the highway.

The problem is not restricted to any one part of the world. Juvenile delinquency, not to speak about juvenile crime, has become almost an accepted part of the everyday scene across the globe. Many officials, teachers, sociologists, social workers, and officers detailed to deal with juvenile problems have confessed that the enormity of the situation has just about reached the point where it is not only beyond their comprehension but beyond their power to supply a corrective except the most drastic and stringent application of laws designed originally to curb hardened criminals and keep them from wrecking society. A supervising sociologist for the Illinois Youth Commission told the 28th annual Illinois Governor's Conference on Youth and Community Service: "To date, we have to admit that to face this problem realistically is to try to keep the conduct of young people within tolerable limits."

Where do young people get the idea that they are responsible to no one but to themselves? Subject to no authority other than the dictates of their own wants and desires? Without the necessity of conforming to any standard, and answerable to no one for what they are and how they conduct themselves? More often than adults care to admit, the problem must be laid squarely at the door of fathers and mothers who have washed out on their responsibilities and have become zoo keepers instead of parents.

When parents no longer recognize children for what they are, gifts of God made by Him and made for Him—to serve Him with all the magnificent capacities they have as human beings —they get what they ask for: little animals with all the instincts of the jungle. The failure of parents to accept children for what they are probably accounts for the growing number of instances where small children have been physically abused by their own parents. Babies are brought into hospitals with broken bones, and X rays very often reveal a number of previous serious injuries. In one case, a three-year-old girl had sustained over a dozen fractures during the course of her short life, all caused by the brutality of her mother. A New York doctor estimated that there are 10,000 cases of serious child injury due to parental brutality in the United States each year. The public is incensed by this news, but it is not similarly aroused by another parental neglect and insensitivity that causes a great deal more damage to the fabric of society—the failure of parents to provide that spiritual upbringing which will help boys and girls become the men and women God intends them to be.

I know men who spend a great deal more time and are much more interested in training a good hunting dog than in raising the boys and girls God has given them. There are women who are more careful about the cat than they are about their children. Animals in the zoo receive elaborate, expensive, highly scientific treatment. The right temperature and humidity are always maintained in their enclosures. They are provided with the right kind of food, even though it must be flown in from a considerable distance at great expense. One duck-billed platypus in the Bronx Zoo has to have a special type of worm flown all the way from Australia. Animals are given vitamins, shots, antibiotics, and the best care science can provide. Competent veterinarians are on call at all times. No expense is spared to keep a rare animal in a healthy condition. Duck-billed platypuses, however, don't go to Sunday school, and chimpanzees don't listen to Bible stories. These are animals in a zoo, who fulfill their destiny, such as it is, when they are in shape to be viewed by a curious public.

All too many fathers and mothers look on themselves today as glorified zoo keepers, whose business it must be to fit out their charges with tawny coats and the latest hair-do in order that they may make a good impression whenever on public display. Parents become zoo keepers when fathers are only providers and mothers only cooks; when mothers are more interested in dancing lessons than they are in the kind of woman their little girl is going to be; when fathers are more concerned about the college their boy is going to attend than the kind of man he will turn out to be.

To a young man who was almost like a son to him, St. Paul wrote: "Continue thou in the things which thou hast learned and hast been assured of, knowing of whom thou hast learned them; and that from a child thou hast known the Holy Scriptures, which are able to make thee wise unto salvation through faith which is in Christ Jesus."

This young man, Timothy, was not a delinquent. From everything we know about him and from St. Paul's remark about his upbringing, it is safe to assume that he was a young man of mature promise. He got this way not suddenly or spectacularly, not through a momentary emotional experience or a dramatic reversal of his former life, but through continued instruction of the right kind ever since he had been an infant. His parents, or at least his mother and grandmother, did not regard their little boy as an animal. They took him for what he was, a gift of God endowed with all the qualities God has bestowed on the crown of His creation. If a boy is going to become a man, those qualities that make a man have to be developed in him from the moment he is born. Certainly, those notable qualities that distinguish the man from the beast cannot be ignored in this process. Man is not a man unless he has been educated to serve the God who made him, the God who redeemed him in Jesus Christ, and the God who will one day invite him to the kingdom prepared from the foundation of the world for those that love Him.

Children should not be underestimated. The minds of little children, like wet cement, are capable of receiving and retaining deep impressions. Trained in the right way from little on, children are capable of complete trust, thoroughgoing honesty, and unconditioned love. Children can receive the gift of God's Holy Spirit and the covenant of God's love. Very often they understand better than adults what our Lord was talking about when He said: "Ask, and it shall be given you; seek, and you shall find; knock, and it shall be opened to you" (Matt. 7:7). Children can pray with a whole heart.

It is almost criminal to neglect the spiritual

life of a child. Yet many parents feel that when they have given their children clothing, food, shelter, medicine, and education, they have given them everything. Such people are not parents; they are zoo keepers. They could do just as well with a duck-billed platypus when it comes to fulfilling their God-given destiny as parents.

St. Paul was not living in a fool's world. He knew what was going on around him: "Evil men and seducers shall wax worse and worse, deceiving, and being deceived. But continue thou in the things which thou hast learned and hast been assured of, knowing of whom thou hast learned them; that from a child thou hast known the Holy Scriptures, which are able to make thee wise unto salvation through faith which is in Christ Jesus."

Here is a plan and a program to fight juvenile delinquency. It calls for reform, not so much on the part of children as of parents. It is an ongoing program, beginning early and continuing late. It is not spectacular, but it works. It is not the product of a mystical dreamer, but something practical that can be carried out in every home. "Train up a child in the way he should go, and when he is old he will not depart from it." (Prov. 22:6)

While I do not despise the religious training given boys and girls in church and school, I would have you note that St. Paul is talking here about the training of a boy at home. If there is no respect for the Bible at home, parents need not be surprised when their boys and girls get out of hand away from home. The Bible has something to say to boys and girls, something that, taught at home, will stand them in good stead when they are away from home and as long as they live.

Boys and girls are well off who learn at home what their parents expect of them. Especially fortunate are those boys and girls whose parents make it clear that what they expect has been drawn from the Word of God, the Holy Scriptures. Here is the authority of God Himself speaking to men—to parents that they may be worthy of their high calling, and to boys and girls that they may become dutiful sons and daughters, not only of their parents but of the living God.

This program is no mere formality. It is not a question of just reading a chapter of the Scriptures from day to day. Timothy learned the Holy Scriptures, what they have to say to every one of us in the ordinary affairs of life. From the Scriptures he received not just a formal training but an education of the mind, heart, and soul, leading to a great end: faith in Christ Jesus. "From a child thou hast known the Holy Scriptures, which are able to make thee wise unto salvation through faith which is in Christ Jesus."

Atheists in communist Russia appear to understand this principle of education a lot better than many people in the Western World who consider themselves religious. Communists keep insisting that anti-God teaching must be begun early if it is to have any effect. One public school teacher in Moscow has said: "Our pupils can still choose to believe in God when they leave school, but it has never happened in the 27 years I have been a teacher." If they are going to be zoo keepers, at least the communists propose to do the job thoroughly.

If boys and girls are going to become real men and women, a credit to their parents and faithful to their God, they have to be educated that way. No better method has ever been proposed in the history of the world than the one laid down in this text: "Continue thou in the things which thou hast learned, knowing of whom thou hast learned them; and that from a child thou hast known the Holy Scriptures."

If this program were followed out, juvenile delinquency would be rare indeed. Religion is caught, not just taught. Children catch it from parents who do not teach them one thing and act out the opposite; who do not just send their children to Sunday school and church but bring them in the fear of the Lord; who do not just go through the formalities of religious training but impart the whole spirit of the Gospel to their children with complete understanding of the fact that the Scriptures have a purpose – to make their children wise unto salvation through faith which is in Christ Jesus.

Extensive survey has demonstrated that when parents merely send their children to church rather than *bringing* them, only 20 percent remain faithful throughout their lives. When parents *bring* their children to church, over 80 percent remain faithful.

In many cases, emotional problems of adults reflect the spiritual vacuum of their childhood. When a child is brought up in the nurture and admonition of the Lord, the home is a chapel in which faith is not only confessed but acted out in everyday life. Here you have the makings of a healthy adult. What is more, you have the makings of a citizen of heaven. Holy Scriptures have a purpose: "to make wise unto *salvation* through faith which is in Christ Jesus."

At the heart of the salvation that the Scriptures bring to the heart of a child through faith which is in Christ Jesus is the forgiveness of God, making right everything that has gone wrong. God forgives for the sake of Christ. Faith in Christ accepts this forgiveness, and it goes on from there. Faith gives purpose and power to life, even the young life of a boy or girl. Faith does what harsh correction often cannot do; it puts a boy or girl on the right track.

Curing juvenile delinquency is a complicated

and tough problem. I am talking today about preventing juvenile delinquency. An ounce of prevention, in this case, is worth a pound of cure.

You young people who have just founded a new home, you young men and women who are contemplating marriage, think on these things. Under the blessing of God, you are going to be parents. Be parents, not zoo keepers. Parenthood is a tremendous responsibility. It starts the moment a child is on the way, and it doesn't stop when a child is grown up. Get ready for that responsibility now. Next week, next month, or next year may be too late. Be the kind of man or woman God wants you to be, wise unto salvation through faith which is in Christ Jesus. Capture that faith at the altar erected in your own home to the living God through inspiration drawn from the Holy Scriptures. Let the Word of God speak to you as parents, that you may be ready to bring up boys and girls who know where they stand in relation to you and to the God whom you serve. Help them be the kind of boys and girls who will understand what St. Paul is talking about when he says: "Continue thou in the things which thou hast learned and hast been assured of, knowing of whom thou hast learned them; and that from a child thou hast known the Holy Scriptures, which are able to make thee wise unto salvation through faith which is in Christ Jesus." Make up your mind now to be parents, not zoo keepers.

7

Faith and Science

"God is dead!" This pronouncement was made by Friedrich Nietzsche two generations ago. Apparently either a lot of people have not heard about the death of God, or they do not put much stock in the news.

Indeed, some people who formerly espoused a thoroughgoing agnosticism, either on philosophical or scientific grounds, have begun to wonder. The age that was to introduce the rule of man, where all have bread and God is dead, has given us two world wars fought with a ferocity and producing destruction of life and property on a scale never before known in history. Mankind is in conflict across the globe, with nation pitted against nation, class against class, and race against race.

Making the most of this situation are the communists, who claim science as an ally in their struggle to gain and wield ruthless control over large numbers of people. Finding it in their interest to discard accepted morality, they have had to rule out God as the final arbiter of right and wrong, putting themselves in His place and setting up new standards in the application of which they alone are both judge and jury. They argue that faith in God has been responsible for the unjust exploitation of men and nations. For that reason God must go so that a new world, scientifically organized, may come into being.

That there has been unjust exploitation of people and of peoples cannot be denied. This fact only illustrates the selfishness of man, which permeates even his good intentions as sediment sullies every stream.

Whether for political, professional, or philosophical reasons, there are people who actively foment conflict between faith and science. They will probably insist that the conflict lies in the nature of the material at hand or is due to the methods by which each arrives at its conclusions. They may even object to the wording of the title, "Faith and Science." They would prefer faith *or* science, some rising up to defend faith against the claims of science and others putting up a defense for science against faith.

The two do not go together, we are told. People from both sides will support this thesis—in the name of faith and of science. Sometimes it is difficult to determine whether the argument is between people who are in fundamental disagreement or between people who are so sure they disagree that no examination of the problem is necessary or desirable.

Let's assume for the moment that it is possible to discuss faith and science in the same breath. Most of us are surrounded by the wonders science has given us. You don't have to think of the A-bomb or the H-bomb to be aware of that. Step into your family car, board a transoceanic jet plane, open your refrigerator door, turn on your radio set, or visit your doctor and you are brought face to face with the products of science.

Actually science is not so much the production of things as it is a way of thinking. Science is the expression of man's drive to discover what causes things to happen and what may be done to change those causes to produce beneficial effects. When the car breaks down or the electric toaster quits working, we do not try to find out which evil spirit caused it. We look for natural causes. By observing and experimenting, we try to understand the nature of things and how to use the nature of things for the benefit of ourselves or, possibly, of other people as well.

Science has organized a great deal that was unorganized or poorly organized before. I need to mention only biology, chemistry, physics, and astronomy to illustrate what I mean. Compare the knowledge in these fields available to our children today with what our great-grandparents were able to know a hundred years ago.

Of course, not all the problems have been solved. The fact is that science has created many more problems than it has solved. What I was taught about the atom when I went to school looks quite simple alongside what my children learn about the atom today. The atom is a good deal more complex and there are many more unsolved problems connected with it than we were led to believe. Pushing back the frontiers of natural science has disclosed a whole world of knowledge hardly anyone knew existed that still remains to be tapped.

In spite of all his accomplishments in organizing knowledge about the physical universe in which we live, man still has one big nut to crack—himself! If it were not for man, fission and fusion would not today pose the threat of destruction to civilization and to life itself that they actually do. We have learned to control almost everything else except ourselves. About ourselves we have a host of questions: Who am I? Am I a plant? another form of animal? Why do I live and work? Do I really count? Am I just the subject of research, or am I personally significant? To whom? Who gave me these powers? How shall I use them? Where am I going? Is death the end?

There will be scientists who address themselves to these questions in the serene confidence that they can be answered by science alone, using scientific methods. Other scientists have begun to wonder—and to ask questions: Are there limits to scientific inquiry? Do the limitations of man have anything to say about the limits of his scientific knowledge? Have faith and science been fighting a false battle? Has it been like a family quarrel, where husband and wife get into a mighty argument that prevents them from speaking to each other at least for a time? Later on they look back and wonder why they ever quarreled in the first place.

Faith and science will not meet peaceably until each again feels the need of the other. Please do not misunderstand me. A scientist does not need to believe in God to be a scientist, although I am firmly convinced that no adequate philosophy of science can ignore or exclude God. Nor does a man of faith have to know science in order to understand God and His ways with men. But each—faith or science—contributes, or should contribute, in its own way to that fullness of knowledge which makes for healthy, satisfying living.

I speak not as a scientist or the son of a scientist. Let the scientists confess their own sins. The noted space scientist, Wernher von Braun, speaks for at least some of his brotherhood: "Man's chief problem," he says, "is ethical. Its solution requires, therefore, the right kind of partnership between religion and science. Pride in human achievement kills humility which is the mother of any true scientific progress. . . . Science and scientists should put this simple but widely unknown truth across to people everywhere. With all the modern means at our disposal, with schools, churches, educational institutions, press, radio, and television, we should tell the world that religion and science are not incompatible; that, on the contrary, they belong together." He goes on to say: "Only with God re-instated in the heart of the world will He furnish mankind and its leaders with ethical guidance through the dangers and pitfalls of the technological revolution."

If there have been scientists who refused to recognize their limitations—known authorities on antibiotics have assumed this fact gave them the right to speak with authority on the origin of life—there have also been theologians who in the same way refused to recognize their limitations. So, for example, people who thought they were defending the faith opposed the introduction of anesthesia, bolstering their position with learned arguments from the Scriptures. Later on another theologian pointed out that God put Adam into a deep sleep when He operated on his rib to produce Eve. Only then did a quarrel die that should never have begun.

We Christians leave an entirely wrong impression with people—and especially with scientists—when we read into the Word of God something that God never intended to say.

Some of this confusion arises from mixing

up what the Bible message is and how it was stated originally or should be stated now. The apostles, whose inspired word we have in the Scriptures, spoke to a world that understood the form and size of the universe in very different ways from those we have of understanding it today. They spoke in the language of that time to people who understood both its denotation and connotation very well. When Paul said that the message of faith had gone out "unto the ends of the world" (Rom. 10:18), neither he nor his listeners were thinking of North America, not to speak about South America and Australia.

There is nothing untruthful about Paul's statement. I could not admit that the Holy Spirit ever caused an inspired writer to pen an untruth. What Paul said was true within the context of everything His listeners knew.

God gave His Word to the world in language people knew and could understand. He expects us to understand His Word today—within the context of what we know, which is not so vastly superior to the knowledge of past ages that we cannot grasp what He means to tell us.

God has to condescend to our understanding even now to get through to us. The process He follows can be compared to a father asking his 5-year-old daughter to go upstairs to get his favorite book, *The Life of Christ*, which is lying there together with a number of other books.

77

She would probably not know which book her father meant unless he told her to bring the big bright red book. That she would understand immediately. God wants us to understand. Our grasp of things about us is the alphabet He uses to help us understand His thoughts toward us, which are thoughts of peace and not of evil.

Science as we know it today is largely a product of the 20th century. Ninety percent of all the scientists who have ever lived in the history of the world are alive today. Over 50 percent of all the money spent by the United States on scientific research since the founding of the country was spent during the last 10 years. Science must face the problem of understanding the language of faith, some of it in the Hebrew of 1,500 years before Christ and some of it in the Greek of the first century of the Christian era. Men of faith face the equally difficult problem of bringing to people of the 20th century the Word of God —unchanged and unchanging—in language they can understand today.

The argument between science and faith cannot be dismissed, however, as simply a matter of words or ways of thinking. Faith cannot accept the dictum of some scientists that man is simply the product of evolution and that there is only a quantitative rather than a qualitative difference between him and the animal. Nor can we agree with the naturalistic view that God is merely an idea, the product of man's reason or imagination, subject to change as those abilities develop. We are not misled into thinking that God can be known through scientific research, even though everything else could be known by that method.

God can be known only as He would be known. He can be found only where He would be found. Evidences of His existence and power are certainly apparent in nature, but His own nature is disclosed only in His Word. God's Word culminates and centers in Jesus Christ, His only Son, sent in goodness and love to redeem a wayward and lost world. This is the Gospel of God's grace and glory, and there is no other.

God refuses to submit to a scientific test of His existence or of His redeeming love. Anyone who comes to God must believe that He exists and that He rewards with the knowledge of His grace and glory those who search for Him. This is not hypothesis to be proved by scientific experimentation. It is rather the given, proved by the experience of faith.

A man will not fall in love with a girl by treating her only as an object for study and observation—psychological, physiological, and economic. No one who looks on God as a question mark will ever come to love Him.

Studying the world God has made will not lead you to know Him. This is like studying a love letter written a thousand years ago in another language. By analyzing the writing meticulously, we may come to know when it was written, who wrote it, and possibly to whom it was addressed. But we are not personally involved. While we are preoccupied with this undertaking, a love letter written to us may lie on the table unread and unanswered.

The Gospel of Jesus Christ is God's love letter to the world—the personal expression of His saving will and purpose. In Christ, God has expressed His love to you and all men. His expression took the form of action that all can understand and none dare misunderstand.

Christ is the way to God. He is God's doing. Through the suffering and death of Christ, God has reconciled us, such as we are, to Himself. In Christ, God does not count our sins against us. In Christ, there is new life and hope.

One word to Christian young people thinking about a career in science: Don't worry that science will destroy your faith. The only danger lies in being afraid of growing in your understanding of God and in the knowledge and understanding of the world. Don't put faith in God in a little box somewhere and hide it away. Keep it out there with you at college, in the open. Take Christ with you into the classroom and the laboratory. He is ready to be put to this test. The only question is, Are you?

The foundation of the house of faith in God

is not the beauty of creation or the orderliness of the universe or its mysteries in yet unpenetrated form. The foundation of faith in God is Christ. "Other foundation can no man lay than that is laid, even Jesus Christ."

8

Act Your Age

Ever since Ponce de León's search for the mythical fountain of youth, people have been looking for some magic formula to hide the evidence, if not to stem the tide, of advancing age. Whole industries are devoted to products that will help preserve the illusion of youth in dress, make-up, manner, and physical appearance.

The evidence of advancing years is on every one of us, whether he is 5 or 45. Why should the passage of 50 years make a person less important or less attractive simply because a part of his future already has become a part of the past, and hamburgers and Coca Cola no longer have the appeal they once had? Why do middle-aged men have to be archly flirtatious to maintain the illusion of youth? Why do middle-aged women have to cover themselves with gook in an attempt to appear 20 years younger than they really are? What's wrong with gray hair, attractively done, when the young look upon it with admiration as the mark of an experience they have yet to gain?

For generations, young people have been

told by their parents: "Act your age." Today the young wish they could give the same advice to their elders: "Act your age."

The popular legend is that women are more disposed than men to try to conceal their age. The legend is an old one. When Cicero was told that a certain woman was in her early thirties, he responded that it must be true, because she herself has been saying the same thing for 20 years.

Of course men fear advancing years just as much as women and are just as self-conscious about their age. Recently a pastor in a large American city was making out a charter for his Boy Scout troop. When he asked the various troop leaders their ages, he was met with strong silence. Finally someone suggested that all the committee members be listed as 21-plus. Later on, the pastor discovered that all these leaders actually ranged in age from 27 to 33 years. They were not old people at all—just young people afraid to admit they were no longer teen-agers in the first bloom of youth.

Why this pathological fear of aging? One of the reasons is economics. Discrimination against older people in employment has become so common that to admit one's age almost means the loss of one's bread and butter. In certain parts of the world, it is almost impossible for anyone to find new employment when he is over the age of 40. To act one's age under those circumstances is an invitation to starvation.

The real reason, however, goes a great deal deeper. Failure to act one's age, more often than not, betrays a thorough misunderstanding of life. If life has only a beginning, a middle, and an end, the end becomes all-important. When people spend most of their lives trying to look away from life's end, youth becomes a symbol of immortality and age the symbol of death.

Man is still not able to accept himself for what he is. Like Eve, we still want to be little gods. Trying to be ourselves, without recognition of the God who made us, we become something we are not.

Some pin their faith on science for a solution to the problem. Science has extended the life span and has conquered many diseases. Science stands on the frontier of many discoveries. The lingering hope continues to haunt the heart of man that perhaps a cure for old age and death is just around the corner. Until the world turns that corner, solace will be sought in the pursuit of false youthfulness and in a desperate quest for recreation. Some will endeavor to escape in the fog of alcohol and others in the empty chatter of inane conversation.

While we talk, we are growing older. In a thousand ways we are reminded of the fact. A new wrinkle or a new gray hair, loss of spring in the step or a sagging waistline never let us forget that we are not gods. As little as a tree can ignore its falling leaves or a flower in full bloom can ignore the icy winds, so little can we ignore the signs that the winter of life is always drawing closer.

We can solve the economic and cultural problems associated with advancing age. We can make it possible for older people to secure productive employment. We can venerate age instead of despising it, but the basic problem will not be solved until we understand what life is all about.

A man advancing in years understood life for what it is. Understanding, he accepted the fact that he was growing old. With grace and dignity he addressed the God who had made him a man: "O God, from my youth Thou hast taught me, and I still proclaim Thy wondrous deeds. So even to old age and gray hairs, O God, do not forsake me, till I proclaim Thy might to all the generations to come. Thy power and Thy righteousness, O God, reach the high heavens." (Ps. 71:17-19)

The psalmist found the answer to the yearning of his heart in God. If there is an emptiness in the heart of you older people, your answer is in the God who neither slumbers nor sleeps, keeping watch over His own.

The great God who made the world and all that is therein knows our frame, that it is dust.

Moved by the fact that men must die, God acted. His Son became a man, and His Son died the death of men. Why fear death when the power of death has been forever broken? Jesus Christ rose from the dead and with His resurrection shattered the tyranny of everything associated with death. The thought of death is not a fearsome threat striking terror into the hearts of those who put their trust in Christ.

They have broken out from the prison and no longer belong to those "who through fear of death are all their lifetime subject to bondage." Having got rid of the bondage, they no longer have to worship youth. Nor are they driven by an inner compulsion to try to recapture their youth. They belong to God, and they can act their age.

The fountain of youth they have found is in the quiet harmony of a garden outside the wall of Jerusalem. There, almost 2,000 years ago, the great God disclosed the secret of life — eternal life through faith in the atoning sacrifice of His own Son, Jesus Christ. There everything falls into true perspective, and every man can know what life is all about.

Buoyed up by the constant assurance of forgiveness in Jesus Christ and carried along by the new life in Christ, age requires a glory all its own. In Christ time becomes merged with eternity, and all is well.

If time is everything, it becomes a tyrannical taskmaster. Television programs have to be completed in 30 minutes or an hour. In that short space of time a mystery has to be solved, the villain exposed and punished. If necessary, events have to be telescoped in order to meet the exigencies of time.

God does not work on a 30-minute schedule. He sees everything and acts on everything in the perspective of eternity. As His children, we are not on a 30-minute schedule. We are not even on a schedule restricted to time. We work and live and believe and hope with the perspective of eternity.

"From my youth," said the psalmist, "Thou hast taught me, and I still proclaim Thy wondrous deeds. So even to old age and gray hairs, O God, do not forsake me, till I proclaim Thy might to all the generations to come." No matter how many times the earth revolved around the sun or how weakened his powers might become, this man had a great story to tell. His life had purpose; from the activity inspired by that purpose he would never retire. No one would ever be able to say of him that being old he had become useless. He was carried along on wings of an eagle by the great God, whose power and righteousness reach the high heavens.

Have you ever gone on a long trip, experiencing the wonderful feeling of finally drawing close to your destination? The journey is almost over. Pretty soon you will be with the people who have been expecting you. Life is a journey too. Why should anyone feel bad that the journey is almost over? Why try to hide the fact that you have come a long way? Every day that passes, every night you sleep, you come a step closer to home. Strangers and pilgrims here, the travelers will soon pitch their tents on the other side of the river. You can't settle down now, with your destination so near at hand. Why try to make yourself at home here, when home is there? Why try to play the part of a young man when you are growing older? Why not act your age?

When a soldier returns from long service overseas, his sleeves are filled with what are popularly called "hash marks," the sleeve stripes marking the years of his service. The more sleeve stripes he carries, the more honored a man he is, set apart from the green recruits who have just completed their training in boot camp. The envy of all is the 30-year man whose sleeve stripes almost reach his elbow.

Age has its own hash marks—the bent back, the slower step, the snowy hair. These are the marks of the seasoned veteran, to be worn with pride and distinction. They are assigned only to those who are no longer raw recruits in the struggle of life.

In a different age, a wise man, old in years,

wrote to a young pastor: "Let no man despise thy youth." If the apostle Paul were writing today, I imagine he would have had to say to some older man: "Let no man despise thy age." It is a cross-eyed generation that despises a man because of his age. Such contempt, one day, will have its reward. Ironically the people who receive it will have prepared it themselves.

God does not despise age. He honors age. God honored Moses. He took him up on the mountain that looked down on the Jordan River, 3,500 feet below. To this man, along in years, God said: "The land I promised to Abraham and his descendants I have let you see with your own eyes, but you shall not go over there." There Moses died, and God Himself buried the body of the elder statesman. Moses was 120 years old when he died; his eye was not dim nor his natural force abated.

Forty years before, at the age of 80, this man was reluctant to take on another job. But God called him. God could use him. Moses answered the call.

At the age of 80 the greatest work of this man still lay before him. Another greater than he later remarked: "There has not arisen a prophet in Israel like unto Moses."

There is no need to apologize and no occasion to complain because you have reached advanced years. You have come of age in a world that itself has come of age. Where men formerly prided themselves on being able to go around the world in 80 days, a man can go around now in 80 minutes. Still the nations threaten and strut as if they were armed with muskets instead of weapons that can destroy millions. Oceans are no longer insurmountable barriers; the mountains cannot protect us unless they fall on us.

You older people, in a world that has come of age, act your age. This is no time for standing around wringing your hands. Share your wisdom in a kindly way with a perplexed generation. Proclaim the wondrous deeds of God, sure in the faith that to old age and gray hairs He will not forsake you. Proclaim His might to the generations to come.

Let the young know, with a light in your eyes and a smile on your face, what it means to belong to God, giving them hope for the day when age will steal upon them. Say to the young: "When the mountains are worn down and the worlds are crumbled to dust, when the hottest star is a cold cinder and the galaxies are no more, I shall stand before God's face clothed in eternal youth. When the endless light-years have faded out and the light of eternity has dawned, life will scarcely have begun. So why be afraid of growing old? The best is still to come!"

9

The Communist Religion

Count your pulse for the next 10 seconds, and you will have the number of new babies born into the world during that time. People are still dying, of course, but not nearly as fast as people are being born. During this year, about 50 million people will be added to the population of the world—in other words, about as many as constitute the entire population of France.

Each of these children as he grows up will attempt to find answers to the three great questions of existence: Whence came I? Why am I here? Whither am I going? The answers he finds will constitute the faith by which he lives.

About a third of the increase in the world's population this year will be contributed by the people of the Republic of China, communist Red China. Their children, along with millions of others in lands under communist domination, will be invited and even compelled to accept the answers of communism to the age-old questions regarding human existence.

Communism is not just a political theory or an economic system. It is a religion that does not pretend to be anything but a religion. Even the controversies among the communist elite are characterized by religious terms: orthodoxy, heresy, dogmatism, and sectarianism. These are terms used in *Pravda* to describe the current communist line or deviations from it.

The creed of communism has been described by the communists themselves as "dialectical materialism." With dialectical materialism the communist leaders from Marx, Engels, and Lenin on down to the present time have attempted to answer the questions of human existence. They say: "Do you want to know why there is so much misery in the world? We can tell you. Do you want to do something about it? We have a philosophy that unites thought and actions. Do you want hope? We promise you the perfect rule of man."

As Marx and his followers look at history, there have always been those people who are forced by economic necessity to rob and deprive the worker of the justifiable results of his labor. Workers have always struggled to achieve their place in the sun, but as one order fell to another, they have always been cheated of the promised goal. In every case this happened because workers did not realize what was being done to them or were unable to discern the true cause of the world's ills.

Communism teaches that once a worker realizes that he is only a material being and that all the thoughts and values in the world have been shaped by economic forces, he will rise up, form a classless society, and achieve matchless happiness.

As communists interpret history, religion has always been used to foil the worker. For that reason, the very concept of God must be erased from the worker's mind. As Marx put it: "Religion is the opiate of the people."

Communist theory holds that when the very idea of God has been discarded and a new communist world order has been established, men living under this system will be altogether unselfish, loving, and peaceful. Under pure communism, therefore, there will be no further need for government, and heaven will have been introduced to earth under the slogan, "From each according to his ability, to each according to his need."

There have always been arguments in the communist camp as to whether it will be possible to introduce the new communist order while certain countries are still living under the system of capitalism, which the communists usually describe with such adjectives as dirty, devilish, and fascist. The devil in the new communist religion is capitalism, producing all manner of degeneracy. Consequently it is impossible for communist man to deal with capitalist man, a fact that justifies for communists the radical and brutal

93

extermination of people within their own countries who still preserve the decadent ideas of private enterprise, the right to own property, and civil righteousness under just law. To be committed to anything other than communism is the greatest sin, and "the wages of sin is death."

The transition from capitalism to communism is supposed to be accomplished by socialism. Under socialism, as communists understand it, the means of production, and indeed all property, are to become the property of the state under communist direction.

The price paid by people who either accepted or were forced to accept this communist interpretation of life has been fearful. The price, Marx frankly stated, would have to be the violent overturn of existing regimes. Lenin added that violent revolution would have to be followed by bloody dictatorship in brutally naked form.

Communist idealism concerning the future has been largely overshadowed by grim dictatorship, such as has been in force in Russia for over 40 years now. Communist dictatorship follows the laws of other dictatorships. The ruling group, fearful and insecure, deals ruthlessly with every sign of opposition. The terror that always accompanies a communist revolution has been woven into the very fabric of the communist political system. Inspiring all of it is the communist religion, calling for total commitment of the whole

94

person and of every person who voluntarily lives or involuntarily is forced to live under the communist system.

Once they have achieved power, communists think nothing of torturing people in order to make them act against their conscience. Their evident purpose is to destroy every vestige of moral integrity in order to establish their own system of morality. As an official Russian publication puts it: "From the point of view of Communist ethics, only what aids the destruction of the hated features of the bourgeois, of the old capitalist world of exploitation and poverty, only that which goes to build the new Soviet socialist order is moral and tenable."

By that definition, anything goes as long as it is communist in origin and communist in motivation. Joseph Stalin, for example, may have been a sadistic murderer who tortured women and children in order to accomplish his objectives, but he was a good Marxist whose methods can be forgiven in view of his objectives. That statement comes not from me but from Mr. Nikita S. Khrushchev in his speech to the 20th Congress of the Communist Party held in the Kremlin.

On the one hand, communists have disregarded the demands of truth and have swept aside the individual rights of man. On the other hand, with nothing less than religious fervor they have proclaimed themselves the saviors of man from exploitation and poverty, the apostles of a new and perfect society. Since there seems to be such a definite contradiction between their purpose and their methods, how is it that communist preaching and teaching have produced such remarkable results as communist domination over 800 million people on this globe?

The results are actually not so remarkable when one considers the ground in which communism does its work. Communism preaches materialism to nations not now communist who have given themselves over to a thoroughgoing materialism. What about our own standards of success? Isn't success determined among us largely by the size of a man's salary, the kind of car he drives, the club to which he belongs, or even the church of which he is a member? Is this the reason that uncommitted nations, looking at communism and at us, find it difficult to choose between communism and our own way of life?

We are shocked at communism's claim that man has no need of God and that God is but an invention of man to explain the things he cannot otherwise explain. Has this attitude been advanced only by communism? In his book *The Witness*, Whittaker Chambers (himself a former communist) says that the choice today is basically a choice between God and man, and the communist has chosen man. In so doing, Mr. Chambers points out, the communists have taken the logical step, "which three hundred years of rationalism hesitated to take, and what millions of modern minds think but do not dare or care to say: if a man's mind is the decisive force in the world, what need is there for God? Henceforth man's mind is man's fate."

Can we dismiss as unexplainable the fact that communism, with its zealous preaching against misery and its fervent belief in a perfect rule of man, should be occupying the place in life that the Christian religion once held? The rise of communism could very well be the judgment of God on the Christian church and on Christian people who have failed to make clear their Christian concern for the grinding poverty of their fellowmen and have failed to proclaim the Christian hope in its full glory.

The answer to communism cannot be found in ridicule of the communist religion or in trying to excuse the injustices that have gone under the name of Christian by simply pointing out the black deeds of communism. The answer to communism is not to give up on Christianity, which would be to agree with the communists that Christian faith is hopelessly antiquated.

The answer lies rather in holding up our own materialism, pride, and irreligion, our own lack of Christ-like love, to a closer examination. At its best, Christian faith has never been unwilling or afraid to do just that. Communism denies that there is evil in man, taking the optimistic view that the right economic system will create right-minded people. Christian faith does not go for that kind of self-deception. It recognizes the existence of evil in the world, calling men to repentance for their sins and to faith in God.

Christian faith is at war, described by St. Paul in these realistic words: "We are not contending against flesh and blood, but against the principalities . . . against the world rulers of this present darkness, against the spiritual hosts of wickedness in the heavenly places." (Eph. 6:12)

St. Paul was talking not just about developments like communism but about the satanic forces seeking to dethrone God from the hearts and minds of men. St. Paul followed up his statement of the problem with a clarion call to action: "Wherefore take unto you the whole armor of God, that ye may be able to withstand in the evil day and, having done all, to stand. Stand, therefore, having your loins girt about with truth, and having on the breastplate of righteousness, and your feet shod with the preparation of the Gospel of peace; above all, taking the shield of faith, wherewith ye shall be able to quench all the fiery darts of the wicked. And take the helmet of salvation, and the sword of the Spirit, which is the Word of God; praying always with all prayer and supplication in the Spirit, and watching thereunto with all perseverance and supplication for all saints." (Vv. 13-18)

Communism offers its answer to the problems of mankind in the gospel of Marx. Christian faith finds its answer to the problems of mankind in another Gospel, in that of St. Mark, where Jesus of Nazareth rises up to say: "The kingdom of God is at hand; repent and believe the Gospel."

This is a revolutionary Gospel. It disavows materialism as an acceptable way of life and calls to faith in the living God. It tells of God's remarkable act in sending His own Son, Jesus Christ, to be the Savior of the world. Christ came with healing power, caring for the sick and the poor, teaching that henceforth whatever men did for the unfortunate by faith in Him, they did for Him.

Christ shared the loneliness and the homelessness of men. He shared their life and their death. The death He died was that of a common criminal. All this is historical, not theoretical. On Christ's life, death, and resurrection from the grave is based the Christian manifesto: "He died for all, that they which live should not henceforth live unto themselves, but unto Him which died for them and rose again." (2 Cor. 5:15)

In Christ, states the Christian manifesto, there is peace with God and the possibility of peace with one another. In Christ the old transgressions are forgotten, the old antipathies put away, the old contempt for one's self and for others removed. In Christ there is resurrection to a new life right here and now, a life that will one day be revealed in all its glory.

Christ did not turn His back upon our world; neither can we. The ultimate dignity conferred upon our humanity is that He became one of us and remains one of us. If by dying He redeemed us, it is incumbent upon us to live as the redeemed children of God — to be good neighbors in factory or field, not merely in church or chapel.

We Christians must believe — not in tranquilizers or in self-helps promoting emotional security, but in the living God. We must worship Him with a heartfelt "Thy will be done!" We must quit thrusting God out to the fringe of life and put Him at the center of our lives. We must look upon God not as a convenient tool but as the almighty Lord He really is.

Uncommitted Christians are as great a danger to what we stand for as communism. "Nothing is more dangerous to true Christianity, nothing more contrary to its nature," wrote Kierkegaard, "than to get men to assume light-mindedly the name of Christian, as if it were something that one is as a matter of course."

The Christian faith has a great message to proclaim and a great responsibility to fulfill. Why should we feel pessimistic and uncertain, when God has promised to be on the side of those who fervently trust in Him?

Christian faith has in its hands a method to conquer the world. That method is love. This weapon is not found in the communist arsenal. Love comes alone from God, who first loved us. Brethren, "if God so loved us, we ought also to love one another."

Communists do not know what love is! They cannot know, because they do not know God. They offer people equality and justice, but actually substitute one kind of oppression for another. Love is Christian—Christian faith in action. We cannot put faith into action by being one-legged Christians. To put faith into action, we must be active in love, bringing to people everywhere that liberty with which God has made us free.

Let us make no mistake about it: We are in a fight to the finish. The conflict, in the last analysis, is not between the people of the free world and the people under communist rule. It is between God and Satan, both of whom have followers on both sides of the Iron Curtain. It must be our business with God's Word to break through the curtain on both sides of the Iron Curtain.

It is our faith that Christ is unconquered and unconquerable. In Him we have put our trust, and in Him is our hope.

Saints and heroes long before us
Firmly on this ground have stood;
See their banner waving o'er us,
Conquerors through the Savior's blood.
Ground we hold whereon of old
Fought the faithful and the bold.

Fighting, we shall be victorious
By the blood of Christ, our Lord;
On our foreheads, bright and glorious,
Shines the witness of His Word;
Spear and shield on battlefield,
His great name we cannot yield.

10

The Government of God

A man once told Dwight L. Moody that he had no interest in an approaching election in his own country. "My citizenship," he remarked, with a good deal of piety, "is in heaven." The well-known evangelist replied: "Brother, you had better get your citizenship down to earth for the next ten days."

Since Christianity is essentially a religion to prepare men for heaven, a fact that St. Paul continually emphasized, people asked the apostle why he laid such stress on behavior in this world. Paul replied in the thirteenth chapter of the Epistle to the Romans: "Because, as I think you have realized, the present time is of the highest importance — it is time to wake up to reality. . . . It is important that we be Christ's people from head to foot," in every relationship of life, including our relationship to government. (Vv. 11, 14)

The thirteenth chapter of St. Paul's Epistle to the Romans, along with a number of other passages in the New Testament, underlines the responsibilities Christians are expected to assume as citizens of the country in which they live.

Though their faith may be other-worldly, Christians are expected to take an active part in the life of the world round about them, a world that is under the governance of the same God who has extended His grace to the world through Jesus Christ.

Government, writes the apostle, is of God. "Let every person be subject to the governing authorities. For there is no authority except from God, and those that exist have been instituted by God." (V. 1)

St. Paul lived under a dictatorship, which can be a most tyrannical and oppressive form of government. He was not giving his blessing, however, to this or any other form of government as if it were God ordained above all others. He was simply stating the fact that God exercises His authority in the world through the institution of government. Whatever form government may take—and it has taken some mighty strange forms in the hands of willful and irresponsible men —still it stands under the judgment of God and is legitimate only by virtue of the fact that its authority is derived from God. This is true even of those forms of government where the governing authorities receive their powers through the consent of the governed. God still rules, and His authority in the last analysis is the only authority. "There is no authority except from God, and those that exist have been instituted by God."

If there were no wrongdoing, no crime, no challenge to God's authority, there would very likely be no need for government—at least not for the kind of government that is necessary in our kind of world, the kind of which St. Paul speaks in this chapter.

If people are going to live with each other in some peace and security, a check has to be put on the coarse outbreaks of violence and lawlessness. God Himself has put that check on these outbreaks through the divinely established institution of government. Because government checks the natural course of sin and selfishness, thus permitting men to live together in a certain degree of harmony—though the tensions of human life often make this an uneasy harmony—government can be looked on both as a means whereby God punishes men for their sins and as a vehicle for His divine blessing. Indeed, one of the greatest punishments God can inflict on a country is to give it a weak and ineffectual or a tyrannical and arbitrary government—one that acts in a manner contrary to the way in which God wants government to act.

God looks on government not as a master but as a servant. Wherever government fulfills its true function, it is God's servant for the good of mankind. God has given government the responsibility of protecting law-abiding citizens and punishing those who break the law. God

105

never instituted government as a means whereby unprincipled officials might get rich through graft and corruption. The history of mankind is the sad story of how dishonest men at various times have used public office for their own selfish ends, have tried to thwart God's will, and have used His own institution to accomplish the opposite of what God intended.

True government, whatever form it may take, must be a government of law. Law, in turn, has no validity unless it is based ultimately on the law by which God Himself governs the universe. Even if we were to be guided only by human history and experience, it would be perfectly clear to us what this law is for individuals, for the family, for the community, for the nation, and for society as a whole. It calls for honor and respect to parents; it demands regard for the inviolability of a neighbor's person, his property, his rights. Every man enjoys this claim to respect for his person, his property, and his rights not by virtue of the fact that he is a man but by virtue of the fact that he has been created by God. Wherever you look in this world, you come face to face with God. The apostle wants to make it clear that when we are confronted by government we come face to face with God.

Government can fulfill its function as the servant of God only when there is respect for law on the part of its citizenry. That is why St. Paul called upon Christians to show that kind of respect: "Let every person be subject to the governing authorities." He went on to say that Christians are to obey and not to avoid punishment, for the sake of conscience: "You should, therefore, obey the authorities, not simply because it is the safest but because it is the right thing to do" (v. 5). In their relationship to government, Christians are to remember that they owe obedience to lawful authority not simply as a matter of convenience but as a duty to God.

Many people who consider themselves honorable citizens break traffic laws and other regulations without a thought of the obligation they owe to God. Apparently they say to themselves: "This is merely a law; others break it—why shouldn't I?" St. Paul urges Christians to say to themselves: "This is not merely a law; if I disregard this established authority, I'm acting contrary to the will of my heavenly Father. I'm not merely breaking a law; I'm breaking faith with my God."

Christian respect for authority extends beyond the office holder and beyond his office. It extends to God Himself, who has established the institution of government as His way of keeping men under control—men who naturally may not like to be controlled—in order that His authority may be maintained in the world.

Respect for authority, St. Paul made clear, extends to those who are in authority. We may not think very highly of the personal integrity of some office holders, of their family, or of their political associations; yet we must remember the source of their authority. That authority comes from God, and they are "divinely appointed to inflict God's punishment upon evil doers." (V. 4)

There is no real dignity in refusing to acknowledge authority. Even the Lord Christ, the Ruler of heaven and earth, stood before Pontius Pilate and recognized him as judge. One of the curses of our modern world is the lack of reverence for authority, the spirit of rude impudence and lawlessness that is destroying the spirit of people in many lands and corrupting especially the young people of our world.

To respect authority is not to fear it. Are you afraid when a police car trails you on the highway? Obey the traffic laws, says St. Paul, and you will have no need to fear. If an officer of the law should knock at your door today, would you be frightened? If you are following out Paul's instructions, you need have no fear. Would you be afraid if you received a letter from the collector of revenue, questioning you about apparent tax evasions? St. Paul offers the best way to avoid that kind of fear: "Do that which is good."

The apostle writes: "For the same reason you should also pay taxes, for the authorities are ministers of God, attending to this very thing. Pay all of them their due, taxes to whom taxes are due, revenue to whom revenue is due." (Vv. 6-7)

It is in the matter of paying taxes that people are most inclined to resent the whole apparatus of government. This is particularly true when taxes are high, as they are in so many countries of the world today. High taxes would not be nearly so intolerable if governments did not spend money with such wild abandon as they so often do. However, government extravagances are no excuse for dishonesty. Two wrongs can never make a right. Even when government officials play fast and loose with our tax money, Christians are under the obligation to play the part of good citizens.

Good citizenship requires of Christians that they take an active role in government. Good men sometimes say: "Politics is a dirty game; I'd rather have no part of it." Sin is a dirty game too; thank God that Christ did not stay out of it. His supporters deserted Him in droves, until finally He faced the enemy alone on a battlefield named Golgotha. Christians can never forget the battle He fought and the victory He won there — a victory that gave them freedom from sin and its power. Because of Jesus Christ, Christians are free, free to live as His followers, no matter what the form of government under which they live and no matter what the circumstances under which they live. No tyrant can ever take that freedom away.

Christians are free to live as Christians, obeying the highest law of all, the law of love. Listen again to St. Paul: "Owe no man anything, but to love one another. The man who loves his neighbor has obeyed the whole Law in regard to his neighbor, for the commandments 'Thou shalt not commit adultery,' 'Thou shalt not kill,' 'Thou shalt not steal,' 'Thou shalt not covet,' and all other commandments are summed up in this one saying: 'Thou shalt love thy neighbor as thyself.' Love hurts nobody. Therefore, love is the answer to the Law's commands."

Government is God's institution to control people from without, to keep them from doing the things they ought not to do. Christian faith is God's way of controlling people from within, so that they want to do the things God wants them to do.

The Christian life is not hemmed in on every side by a set of laws but is controlled by one law that for everyone who believes in Jesus Christ is the center of his being: the law of love. When things are right at the center, things of the circumference will take care of themselves. You don't have to go out and pick the old leaves off the trees in the forest. God arranges things so that the new sap and the new foliage will throw off the old life. God doesn't have to order Christian parents to take care of their children. He puts love into their hearts, and everything else

110

takes care of itself. God doesn't have to give Christians a set of rules governing their relationship to government. He pours out His love into their hearts, and love takes charge of all their attitudes.

Communism seeks control over the masses of the world by trying to stir up hate and revolution. Christian faith and love have an altogether different objective. They take hold of the heart of a man and make of him a new person. In the apostolic age, Christian faith laid the law of love upon the life of the slave as well as that of the master. It exacted an obligation of love from the master as well as from the slave. And the result was the greatest revolution in the history of the world. In that kind of atmosphere, where faith and love rule, society is blessed, government is recognized as the institution God intends it to be, and freedom becomes not a name but a divine reality.